Law of Position
A Position Location Theory
Delridge L. Hunter, Ph. D, MSCMH, CRC

Department of Social and Behavioral Sciences
School of Liberal Arts and Education
Medgar Evers College
The City University of New York
1650 Bedford Avenue
Brooklyn, New York 11225
347/419/5132
01/21/2017

<<<A Continuum>>>

Law of Position: a Position Location Theory

Abstract

The Law of Position, a Position Location Theory, uses the premise of the Laws of Form as the basis of the numerous axioms that make up this paradigm. Each axiom contains a set of theorems that explain the rules of crossing, calling ((naming) and location (position) as operational forms within a polity of culture. Each axiom is layered to complement and support the others with axioms containing the rules that define distinction as an operational form of inequality. The two, operational processes here that explain the system are crossing and calling (naming). The position theory as a location theory, applies crossing and calling as indicators of the distance between the least favored and the most favored positions. The form of distinction as the original form establishes the motive for the creation of operational barriers to keep the other forms of distinction from crossing. To indicate what forms are to be distinguished from the original form, a name is to be attached to each form to inform that particular, what value is assigned to that name called. The name called and called again establishes that name as an indication of what form of distinction it is.

The discourse seldom uses the word "location" because it is implied every time the word "Position" is used.

A Time of Discovery

While employed as an Expediter, at the H. Singer Zone Center in Rockford, Illinois from 1966-1969 I was introduced to a new theoretical construct called "Position Theory." Position Theory, I was told, was never written down by the author, a well respected clinical social worker, but it was well known within his institution because he taught it to his graduate students. After learning how he applied the new construct, I found the name useful in understanding other definitions of social arrangements. It may be applicable to almost every thing constructed.

Position Theory immediately resolved the problematic with theoretical constructs based on race/color/class, nationality/religion/creed, and gender/gender relations. As I now understand the theoretical frame, Position Theory applies to anything that has itself as its own particular while operating as part of a whole. Position with its broad and deep connotations in usage is a simple equation that can operate on any level or with anything, i.e., it can apply to any form of distinction.

In listening to my informants it was immediately revealed how Position Theory may inform my effort to understand the competition in complementarities of an open society by adapting it to the study of social intercourse. Position Theory [location] as applied here is an integrated process that involves applying many fields of study or disciplines simultaneously as one.

Prior to the development of integrative study more often than not research and instruction involved an examination of a piece of things or activities that happened in particular past, or after the fact, as a disciplinary, i.e., taken from the whole, a part/piece of) research or instructional procedure. No other ways of researching social forms was deemed legitimate: this is empiricism. This means of conducting research and instruction dominated university research for most of the 20th century. As we approach the first decade of the new millennium, the 21st century, the notion of disciplinary learning is no longer considered the only way of receiving a more focused understanding of behavior as it operates within the realm of social intercourse. [1996, C.E.]

The old process of dividing social intercourse into minute parts of study is now informed by integrating the focal points of complementary fields of inquiry. Offering a holistic view of any matter under discussion now complements disciplinary learning. Study in the realm of social intercourse that has developed within the polity of culture offers scholars a new way to examine the interaction between all of the other positions that exist as what I call the least and most favored positions in an open society.

A new paradigm is what the Position Theory has brought to the discussion on social constructs. It was in hearing the name Position Theory that allowed me to move beyond the old theoretical constructs I found wanting. The name position/location applies to anything and anybody, individual, group or any larger configuration thinkable that can be identified by calling the name. Creatively the Position Theory is like Blues, in that, it uses two processes: crossing and calling (naming and re-calling) to serve as the base of any observation made. Blues, the music of (from) Africa, allows any equation as a composition to be rendered simply by starting with three minor tones. Back during the late eighteenth and early nineteenth centuries, one could hear these minor tones played in Blues or any of the forms created out of that form of music.

With Blues serving as the analogy, here is a brief viewing of Position Theory as a working paradigm reflecting the manners or ways and means of Blues Aesthetics.

Position Theory maintains that to use crossing and calling as viable constructs permits scholars to inform their observations by realizing that crossing is a process operational when boundaries have been set and barriers erected. Either one crosses the barrier or one does not. A scholar may observe the activity-taking place as it is in motion during the movement to cross. An observation is made of the activity that is Omni-present and interactive. It allows one to study the position and the process.

Since the process of crossing is ongoing during this attempt to cross over, to learn the value of the crossing of one attempting to get over to the other side, one must know the name with a value attached to the crossing. As the challenge to the person seeking mobility, the crossing must possess a value equal to or greater than the name of the caller. Calling the name of the crossing, i.e., to go over to the other side, that has been named, gives value to the name called. It also shows the greater value assigned to the barrier erected to deny the crossing. The observations of crossing and calling are dynamic processes to be studied.

Social beings are always making adjustments with the knowledge that each has about movements in relationship to the information available about how and when to cross, if crossing is permissible. Crossing and calling have to do with the original mark of distinction made and barriers established by the entity that created the boundary. How a distinction is made and how the boundary is indicated to show a distinction is the role of language. The language that expresses the movement of entropy is what Position Theory allows one to investigate.

The likeness of Position Theory to Blues as a form of distinction is a demonstration of how the Position Theory may be used to inform scholars of what major contributions have been made directly by the least favored people. The information may be taken from the above statements regarding the minor tones. What has come out of the blues form of distinction is the invention of music the evolved into multiple sets that continued to expand. These new musical ideas all emanate from experiences working with three minor tones. The past creative activities are important contributions to the progression and development of world music. However, the contributions are virtually ignored by the dominant culture in the United States.

Applying the Position Theory, to the study of blues forms, allows scholars to see that the application of minor tones has resulted in the fundamental changes in modern music. This major contribution to music resulted from the creativity of the least favored people in society. Yet this music is not exemplified, as having any worth because the form of distinction casts on the contributors is that of the least favored position. Correspondingly, that same music adapted by members of the most favored, i.e., George Gershwin, assume more currency simply because these contributors hold positions as members of the most favored in society. With the George Gershwin analogy, what crossing the boundary has shown is it was only when a member of the most favored found blues in the form of Jazz a musical construct that could inform his work that the music began to receive acknowledgement as an artistic form worthy of listening to, i.e., worthy of recognition. Prior to his intervention, any artistic form emanating from the least favored was denied any crossing, except as the primitive works of a buffoon.

New Thinking Has Emerged

The least favored and the most favored as positions, have allowed me to observe bias as an operational form within the United States and most other polities of culture. However, my design as constructed within the least favored and most favored positions only allowed an application of black and white positions taken from chess. In other words, my initial design outlined the black and white positions as least favored and most favored, but did not advance the notion into a new paradigm until crossing and calling were understood.

The desire was to create a new workable paradigm. There was a need for a new premise supported by axioms. The idea was to create sets in the form of axioms that would offer new ways of examining social intercourse. Now the task was to give new definitions and language to the process.

The design of the Position Theory is to allow scholars to delve into how bias serves as a motive to establish a boundary of distinction in an open society. Must there be a motive for bias to become the ideological form that promotes discrimination? Must there be the intent to harm a particular group for bias to operate? Must there be a motive for one group to name another group that already has a form of indication that it accepts as defining who it is? These are questions pondered after reading chapter 1, Laws of Form. This is getting ahead of the story.

Moving to New York City in 1977 after spending a year in E. St. Louis, six years in Rockford, Illinois, and seven years in Ithaca, New York, I visited all of the bookstores I came across in Greenwich Village, until I happened upon a small intellectual bookstore located on Astor Place between Broadway and Lafayette. What attracted me to the store was the sight of men dressed in European cut suits standing with a book in their hands as they perused these works with great interest. At some point during my visits, I noticed, located on a shelf in the window of the bookstore was a new book entitled, Laws of Form. G. Spencer-Brown, a mathematician/philosopher who taught at Cambridge University, wrote it.

At first I simply stared through the window at the book every time I visited the bookstore and wondered, "Who would write a book on laws of form and call it logic?" I always concluded as I entered the store, "It looks very interesting." Yet, I never looked for it on the shelf for quite some time. Instead, I wandered through the works that I had wanted to examine. I did not want to get side tracked. Eventually, I went to the philosophy section to look for the work to no avail. Not finding it, I approached the person at the counter and said, "Good afternoon, excuse me. Under what section will I find Laws of Form by G. Spencer-Brown?"

I recalled a surprised look of disdain immediately expressed across his body. He said after a great pause, with the obvious disdain still present and never bothering to return the salutation, "Laws of Form can be found in philosophy or mathematics, we have it located in both categories because of the nature of the work," as he turned his body away from his customer. I responded, understanding the tone, the language, and the gesture, "I looked in the philosophy section and it was not there, that is why I came to you, to seek your assistance." He was embarrassed. His bad behavior was so obvious that other customers looked on in amazement as they looked at me to see my response. I smiled at his behavior, shook my head in disbelief, as I walked away from the counter.

I discovered the book in the mathematics section, and did what was custom, tore the cellophane cover away from the brand new book and began to read it. I discovered unlike the other esoteric works there, it was in paperback. Not waiting to read the biographic sketch of the author and/or the review on the back of the book, I began reading the preface. I read it once. I read it again and again until I fully understood what was said. "That was only the preface," I said. "God Damn, this is some heavy doo doo." This is after my first reading. I thought, "Wow, this is interesting and I have not even read the introduction, yet. I could not get past the preface. I had never seen anything like this before. "I've got to buy this book." The price was around $20.00. The book became chapter one. That chapter became my obsession. It became the book. I would recite "We take as given the idea of distinction and the idea of indication, that in order to make an indication one must first make a distinction. We take therefore the form of distinction for the form." "Heavy! Heavy!"

As a catechism, I recited that chapter and verse everyday until rote memory took hold of the concept, the design, and the logic of the two constructs. The dual constructs called crossing and calling became my obsession. The two work in tandem. It is now understood that the notion of how crossing the boundary that is erected to keep someone out allows me to understand what the idea of crossing means under a new construct: the other variable necessary as a protector to crossing is calling. Everything must be called something. Everybody seems to require a name to be recognized by. The name is the indication of how a particular form will be recognized upon being called. What names will that particular person or group be called?

Papers, proceedings, articles, books, etc., on the Position Theory have been delivered at conferences and other gatherings of intellectuals. No matter the forum, it all comes back to chapter one. It is chapter one that retains my attention for the next twenty odd years until I finally get it. All of the time spent pondering the Laws of Form my progress I share with my scholar learners in class. It is apparent that this sharing with my scholar learners over the school years has brought its rewards. The rewards come from having each class read the Laws of Form and the Position Theory and offer their own analyses of the constructs.

Writing the Law of Position

At last, in 2002, I sat down at a Barnes and Nobel bookstore in Poughkeepsie, NY and wrote what became four axioms. The premise plus axioms are what have emerged as a Law of Position, a position theory. A set of questions inform my Law of Position as an explanation of social intercourse as an operational form within the polity of the culture called the United States of America. My basic query is what form of distinction assumed the original and most favored position in the United States prior to it becoming a State.

Questions were developed in 1977-78 while conducting research for my Ph. D. thesis, The Puritan Invention, in Economics of Education, Education Policy Analysis and Africana Studies at Cornell University. My research led me to the Puritans. It was in studying the Puritans Invention that I thought of the idea of a most favored position as a working model for my thesis. [In 1978/79, I read the entire contract of the Massachusetts Bay Colony in old English at the New York Research Library on 5th Avenue and 42nd Street.]

As I read the contract, it becomes apparent that the most favored position is occupied by the European Americans, in the forms of Dutch, French and British, who have established themselves as occupiers of the original and therefore most favored position in the New World Colony to be called "America." Again, in complementarities the slaves from Africa by design will become the occupiers of the least favored position. As it were, the African American will occupy the least favored position while the European American will occupy the most favored position. The Indigenous Peoples who were virtually exterminated remained in the least favored as "insignificant" Historical Others who's Names were to be abused as (a) historical figures (objects).

The forms of indication that will give credence to those forms of distinction as the names they will retain and/or assign themselves as the original and most favored names, e.g., Winthrop and assign to others regarded as not of and less than As a starter, the European American renames himself "White Man" and assumes the name "America" to the United States of America. White now becomes a favored position expressed as a color of Homo sapiens from Europe. The name America will become the abbreviation of the United States of America. That will become the most favored color to represent the people who are superior. He renames the African Negro and all others accordingly. Black becomes the least favored position as a color to represent the people so defined, i. e., inferior. The white man is the "American" while all others are to affix another name to America to indicate that they too are Americans. From the inception of the New World Colony of North America, it has been "America" at the expense of the other Americas: North, Central, and South, Latino, French, British, Indigenous, Asian, and African.

Out of those two questions (p. 6), the Law of Position, a position theory, has evolved. The intent by the use of the first chapter of Spencer-Brown's work is to form the construct as my premise. The purpose is to investigate the forms of distinction and the forms of indication as they may apply within an open society, e.g. North America.

Introduction

The Law of Position, a Position Theory takes its form from the rules of chess regarding the black position vs. the white position. As applied within this context the black occupies the least favored position while the white occupies the most favored. Any appearance of likeness to past or current theories of chess, race/color/class, gender/sex, religion/creed, and other theories as forms of discourse is only coincidental. However, these previously mentioned theories are "positions" that may serve to inform the process of enquiry. One may say that the rules of distinction and indication apply to all of the previously mentioned theories.

How it works is by employing the Law of Position, a position theory, one may consciously apply the rules distinction and indication to any form that shows by name there is an indication of a mark of distinction without having to use the exception rule in the process. The exception rule is applied when those who are formally left out of the process are now included because they are thought of as exceptions: their skill level permits them entry. But, heretofore, they had no privy to enter, the new ability to enter, by a few made them exceptions. They become the Important Men always treated in History. Thus, although the Constitution of the Hau-de-no-sau-nee Confederacy was read with great interest by many of the Founding Fathers, no mention is made of this reading.

The Law of Position does not explicitly intend nor by implication attempt to negate the theories previously stated. Position as used here means a person is according the rules (ideas) of distinction and indication occupy a location or as a location a position. The positions according to these rules emanate from the most and least favored position as applied to chess.

However, in using the Law of Position, one does not have to apply the exception rule to a particular, when that particular fits within a discussion of a construct under any of the above systems of analyses.

A Basic Premise

We take as given the idea of distinction and the idea of indication, that in order to make an indication one must first make a distinction. We take therefore the form of distinction for the form. G. Spencer-Brown, 1979, Laws of Form, 1.

Axiom 1
The crossing indicates the distinction of the boundary.

By drawing a boundary between each group as separate formations, one formation cannot reach the other formation without crossing the boundary that makes a distinction, i.e., when a boundary between groups is set up, one group cannot reach the other group without crossing the boundary that separates them.

Once a distinction is made for each formation, groups on each side of the boundary, being distinct can be identified as different.   There can be no distinction of groups without motive. There can be no motive unless these groups are thought to differ in value. The group that holds the most favored form of distinction is considered to hold the most value. The intent and/or desire of the least favored groups are to cross the boundary into the position occupied by that group. The value assumed by the group wanting to cross indicates the greater value awarded to and assumed by the most favored group.

The group that holds the least favored form of distinction is considered to hold the least value. The intent and/or desire of the most favored group are not to cross the boundary into the position occupied by that group. The value assumed by the group not wanting to cross indicates the lesser value assigned to and imposed on the least favored group. For the least favored group who desires to enter the position of the most favored and then re-enter their own position, it is like they never entered the position of the most favored, at all.

No one from a group outside of the formation of the most favored position is permitted to enter their formation without approval from or by the most favored.

Groups not allowed to enter the position of the most favored are forbidden to enter the space of the most favored position. Forms of distinction are thereby indicated by positions assigned each competing, corresponding and complimentary group outside of the most favored position. Simply put, each group outside of the most favored position occupies a less favored position.

The extreme opposite group to the most favored is assigned and assumed to occupy the least favored position by those more favored.

Axiom 2

Words create the language of indication to describe the form of distinction.

It is through the usage of symbols called words that we establish language as a means of indication of the motive that brings about a form of distinction. It is through the usage of symbols called words that we call the name of each boundary created to separate one form of distinction from another. It is through the usage of words that a language is developed to give name to that form of distinction. It is through the usage of language that we establish how crossing a boundary of distinction is determined or when that crossing is permitted. It is the usage of language that the motive has a basis of expression for a form of distinction that is made. It is through the further usage of language that a distinction made is an indication of motive.

Put differently, a group thus indicated by an expression of the name is also an indication of the value assigned to that group as a form of distinction.

Axiom 3
The distinction of the claim is indicated by the name.

When a particular group is considered the most favored, i.e., the group that occupies the most favored position of distinction among groups, the name the most favored group assumes, can be taken to indicate the value of the group because of the position of distinction it occupies. To assign a particular group value greater than others, different names can be taken to indicate the value of each of the groups so assigned. To call a group by the name assigned or assumed indicates the value of the distinction enjoyed the group so named. To use that name to call the group again means the value is seen in the name called. The value assigned establishes a distinction that is indicated by the name called. The intent of those who occupy the most favored position is to limit those allowed and/or forbidden to use their name because that name is an indication of their more favored position as a form of distinction. Equally, when the name of the group is indicated to express the value of the group the form of distinction is indicated by the name.

In other words, the name is an indication of the degree of value derived by and/or assigned to that form of distinction.

Axiom 4
Principle as an Operational Form Of Distinction
The Inequality Distinction is an Indication of a Form of Inequality

A reminder: We take as given the idea of distinction and the idea of indication and in order to make an indication we must first draw a distinction. We take therefore the form of distinction for the form.

We take as given that the original form of distinction is the first form. Any other form of distinction created after the original form that is not of or from the original form is unequal in value to the original form. We take therefore the original form of distinction as the form that occupies the most favored position with the most value attributed to that position.

Once the first form of distinction has been established and is accepted as the original and most favored position with a boundary surrounding it, a new form with a boundary is established as a separate form of distinction. The boundary of the new form establishes a position of inequality between forms.

What we are contending here is, to create a form of distinction we must establish a boundary that separates the original as the first form of distinction from any other forms of distinction created thereafter. Once a boundary is established between these forms of distinction an inequality of value is assumed to exist between forms.

For a distinction of inequality to be made between each form a name is given to each [form] as a means of indication as to which [form] holds what distinction that is of more or less value than others. That is, for the original form of distinction to be considered different and of greater value because of its originality, for any other form, a name is assigned to indicate the value of that particular form. The value assigned to each form of distinction is indicated by the name chosen to distinguish that form from other forms. Once a value has been designated to each form by name, the name indicates the distinction in value attributed to that form so named. There must be a motive for one occupying the original position to offer names to other forms not considered part of the original form of distinction or of equal value thereof. Once a name is chosen to indicate one form is of greater value than another a motive has been established. A motive to distinguish one form from another by name establishes an assumption of inequality between forms. Once a motive has been established, value assigned each form by the name called indicates that there is an assumed inequality between forms. In other words, all forms of equal distinction carry the same name.

A difference of name assumes that there is difference of form. That difference of form the distinction is indicated by the name given that form. Stated differently, an unequal value is attached to the name as a description of the form whereby difference establishes one called by that name a position that is less favored. This is called a position of inequality, i.e., a less favored position. When a name identifies each member as an equal within the form, i. e., each member has the same access as a possibility. Any additional name assigned to any member indicates that within the form the additional name has a different value assigned.

When different value assigned to a name is of less value than a more favored name a less favored position is established. Here greater access serves as the means of receiving a chance to advance ones position: a lesser degree of access offer less chances or opportunities to advance from a lesser position. This lack of access establishes a dialogical process of denial and non-recognition.

The lesser form of distinction offers less advantage of opportunity to that so indicated. Put differently, those with the greater degree of access receive a greater chance to advance their position, while those with lesser degree of access receive less chance to advance their or out of their position. In an open system whereby fluidity is operational, it is the degree of openness practiced within process that allows fluidity to provide the Least Favored access beyond that offered through fair practices of Affirmative Action.

Where unequal beings of consciousness exist, an inequality of position within the theatre of social intercourse is indicated by the names assigned.

Axiom 5
The Rule of Negation

The Negation Rule is designed to disallow the least favored any advancement of its position. It is also to disallow any advancement out of that position. The rule is to deny the movement of the least favored into any more favorable position. It is to make the attempt at upward mobility ineffective if not invalid. The intent is to break the complementarities of positions that enrage efforts to allow those who occupy the least favored position any desk=re to create growth and development toward re-inventing themselves as a means of upward mobility. Put differently, it is this denial of movement out of the least favored position. Thus, the mark of distinction in this instance allows the negation rule to deny the least favored from crossing the barrier. The inability to cross the barrier allows the naming and the calling of the name to place stigmas on the ones so named, e.g., Negro, Gypsies (Roma People), American Indians (Indigenous People of the Americas). Ad infinite

Naming (Inclusive)

The African renamed Negro is used as an example of a process of negation by assigning a mark of distinction might be located and named to indicate who/what might be identified as people in bondage.
This is a case of the process operating.

Invention of the Negro

The Process

1. People Trafficking

The process of the invention of the Negro began with the People Trafficking of Africans from particular locations that supplied the workers necessary to perform the types of labor required to develop the agriculture, industrial and trade economy at that particular phase of economic development. The man stealing took place within these villages because they housed the types of workers who were needed to perform specific labor tasks. The labor tasks required dictated the skills sought out by the slavers. To steal people arbitrarily or on a whim was too inefficient and costly. So time was spent locating the "tribe" that performed the labor required developing the agricultural, industrial or trade economy.

2. Transporting

The process of the invention of the Negro moved to the second stage with the transportation of the African to the newly named colonized Americas.

3. Processing – Naming

The process of the invention of the Negro moved to the third stage by processing the African as a Negro into the system of bondage with the old Generic name being replaced by a new name, Negro. As the Negro, the people of the old continent no longer have a place of origin that is clearly defined, i.e., there is no Negro Land.

4. Locating

The process of the invention of the Negro moved to the fourth stage with location of the African as a Negro into a colonial place, e.g. New Amsterdam, and living - work space now about to be given the new "Christian" name as an indentured servant.

5. Renaming—A new name for the African person, so-called Negro, a Christian name is the slave's name

The process of the invention of the Negro moved to the fifth stage with the renaming—naming of the Negro as (s) he is given a Christian first name that is to be certified as the official name of that slave.

6. Indenturing (position servitude)
The process of the invention of the Negro moved to the sixth stage with process of servitude being offered as a permanent position of the worker. The name indicates the position the name implies.

7. Enslaving
The process of the invention of the Negro moved to the seventh stage with the name Negro meaning slave and the Christian name meaning that is how that particular slave is to be identified.

8. Enforcing
The process of the invention of the Negro moved to the eighth stage within the boundary being that of a slave established as the holder of the least favored position by law, with the name Negro indicating the boundary that serves to distinguish itself from the others.

The American Indian Construct

The American Indian construct uses that name of a people not thought to have any advancement worthy of being called by their names because they have no civilization. Not knowing that not all people want to live the way they live, and where India is or who the Indians are the name are the only one the European explorers knew to call any people thought to be where they think they are. Later American is added to assure everyone just learning about these people that they are some-place-else. The new information informs everyone that they were located in the Americas not Asia as previously imagined. Never acknowledging that these European voyagers did not know where they were in space and time, they would never state that these people are given the wrong name. They are given names of another people thousands of miles away. The notion is that they are going to keep that name because like the use of the word Negro the name according to C.L.R. James, serves a "commercial" purpose. People from another place should not be disadvantaged by having to learn every name of every ethnic group called "a tribe". As with the name Indian, the name tribe comes from within the European names of what they are at a different point in socio-cultural development. Likening the Indigenous communities to an understanding of how they developed, these people are thought to be at the "primitive" state of development. Thus, treatment of these communities is thought to worthy of the disadvantages placed upon them. Oppression is thought to be commiserate what mark of distinction is applied this group, so named. They are the least favored in the land mass just assumed to be their own decided these rules created under the Doctrine of Discovery or what the Americans call a state's "Manifest Destiny" give the most favored the Privileges and Immunity take and do what they want. For, they are founding a "new world has become the American Dilemma

.

Examples of other names with a Mark of Distinction that are Indicated by these names: tribe, woman, white, black, savage, nigger, fag, dike, Mexican, Spanish, Bi-polar, rifer, ad finite...

Axiom 6
The Privileges and Immunity Clause of the 14th Amendment

The U.S. Constitution states, "No State shall make or enforce any law which shall abridge the privileges or immunities of citizens of the United States." By *de facto* use of (inclusive) this clause of the 14th Amendment written to protect the civil rights of the African American and others has been diverted to offer privileges and immunities to the least favored population that are called " po' white trash, Irish, Spic" etc., under the race construct. Assuming there are races, under the clause the so mentioned, these least favored people become "White" people.

Axiom 7
Catalyst

Location/production/process

A Catalyst offers, supplies, provides, makes possible, the means, the channel, the vehicle, the method, the medium, the mechanism, the access, to crossing the barrier.

Axiom 8
The Fairness Principle [The Catalyst Construct}
The process of applying the catalyst construct
An operational form called affirmative action of the three (3) clauses of the 14th Amendment of the U.S. Constitution.

Under the fairness principle in a system whereby all social intercourse is equal, goods and services are offered at a fair market value. In a market system, it is in games, e.g., baseball, basketball, etc., that fairness may be practiced in its most objective form. Outside of games, fairness assumes that all goods, services and other forms of social intercourse are available to each according to the value held within the market place of supply and demand. Thus, it is only in games that fairness expresses a measure of merit. In other practices of social intercourse, fairness is awarded according to what position one holds. It, therefore, serves as an operational process of inequality between positions. In so doing the social interaction of it supersedes the ability to establish a "level playing field." In current society, that is called Affirmative Action.

Affirmative Action serves as the ways and means of providing access by establishing a process that offers equal opportunity to the least favored under the fairness principle. The motive is to establish a "level playing field," i.e., offering the least favored access to those areas and materials formally denied. In an effort to establish a level playing field access is provided to the Least Favored in the arenas of employment, housing, entertainment, play, education, the arts, civic life, and other ways and means of conducting social intercourse. Affirmative Action becomes the mode and means of measuring quantitatively the actual success rate, i.e., rate of return, of fairness as a practice within a society that employs two forms of distinction: The most and least favored.

With forms of distinction serving as a way of separating those who are most favored from those who are the least favored, equal opportunity moves the least favored no further away from their original position than before. Except for a change in the social order of inequality sustained by bias, fairness cannot be realized applying Affirmative Action as at means to better access through equal opportunity to all citizens (inclusive) of a given jurisdiction.

Affirmative Action operating within the confines of positions of favor, only permits fairness with a definable demonstrated outcome (DDO), e.g., baseball score of 5 to 4, when the process is conducted as games (a play activity) based on quantitative measurements. As an analogy to civil life, measurement on a quantitative level, Affirmative Action offers no quantitative or qualitative changes to show for its effort. There is no objective change in who occupies the least favored. Despite no meaningful change realized by the least favored, opposition to that effort has led the opponents to allege a false premise called reverse discrimination. Reverse discrimination presupposes that those at the bottom of the social scale once given the opportunity to advance will help the neighbors too, so?

A use of reverse discrimination by the least favored becomes a negation of the negation: Only the most favored can engage in reverse discrimination. That is what we call Affirmative Action. Reverse discrimination by the least favored becomes a reversal of the illusive forward movement the least favored have made on their own. Reverse discrimination supposes the power relationship to authority is one whereby the least favored now has power equal to that held by the most favored. That certainly is not how things are.

What the opposition is bringing to light is the appearance of unity among the least favored. Unity is not reverse discrimination. No matter, unity of the least favored is challenged as cheating, a violation of Affirmative Action thus undemocratic, as showing favoritism to members within the group. On the other hand the most favored is expected to choose from within their ranks for upward movement. It is they who must provide open access as a process for Affirmative Action to increase the value of those less favored. Even so, providing access to those previously denied can never completely reverse the discrimination suffered by these groups, as the least favored.

Put differently, the least favored are not in a position to engage in a practice reserved for the most favored: that of allowing an unequal distinction to be made between equals under the law. In effect the socially based, politically enacted inequality practices are not disturbed without a transformation of the market system regardless of allegations to the contrary.

To camouflage denial emanating through bias practice, a process called purchasing power parity (PPP) is offered as a way for creating a virtually level play field. In reality the whole notion of creating a mathematical economic formula for calculating parity as virtual when there is no value change, only sustains the inequality principle between positions involving social intercourse. What PPP does is offer an explanation of the vast differences between the two positions that is in a language understandable to the most favored. [This fore stated narrative can be found in the book, "Culture of Whiteness VS Black Popular Culture: a Law of Position" Amazon Books]

After Thought

Calling and Crossing

What I found interesting in my examination of Laws of Form was how easy it was to label others as exhibiting some disability or disadvantage, e. g., hair or skin color, that allowed them to be grouped with others for discriminatory purposes of who appears to exhibit the same disability or disadvantage. A disability in this instance is something someone else defines as have a displeasing (disabling) appearance (inclusive) thus placing him or her as a disadvantaged.

The disabling appearance as a form of distinction identified is indicated by the name called. By calling those so identified with that name is designed to express the intent of the label, e. g., Negro meaning, from Africa, occupier of the least favored position, i.e., the black position, as in chess.   Location as a Position allows calling one Negro, the Latin word for Black in English, to assume the name to be negative. The name makes the Negro, the person, undesirable, i. e., the negation rule.

The motive for creating such a label is to discriminate against the group so named. Calling the name of those thought deserving of this form of distinction is done so as to identify to the greater community how such groups should be recognized when their name is called.

The intent of calling a group that is less favored by a name that carries disparaging results is to establish a barrier of entrance to the group so named.   On the other side of the equation is the response of members of the group disparaged is to violate the rule, by crossing, the barrier of exclusion. Please recall, in an open society there are always stated rules of entrance and rejection. To overcome rejection, these ways and means of entrance are learned. Thus when a member of group disparaged happens to find ways of crossing the barrier they apply the rules and when successful they enter the new position by the ways and means they learned.

At this point, if entrance sought is not approved of, but serve as no deterrence to the upward mobility, other barriers are erected or set into place to limit entrance to only those things identified as permissible by the more favored groups. Engaging in the search for further entrance additional ways and means are sought out and applied. They are those who succeed, e.g., Miles Davis and Madam Walker, while others have failed, e.g., an African American lyricist who made one hit. In other words, the less favored must thus find other avenues of crossing barriers that constantly appear as the next barrier - called hurdle - to over come.

The intent of erecting further barriers is to never allow, i.e., deny, that member of the least favored to gain enough favors to become a member of the particular most favored group, e.g., as in the case of Princeton University denying Paul Robeson entrance although he graduated Valedictorian of his neighboring High School graduating class. He was admitted to Rutgers, the State University of New Jersey, also a land-grant college. As things happen the least favored university in regard to Princeton was the recipient of a product of the least favored who surpassed the standards necessary for admittance into European culture, yet was denied entrance by the most favored.

For upward mobility in an open society to be realized, there appears to be a design, e.g., entrance to and graduation from a prestigious institution, a desire to enter and availability. Without access, fairness and merit there is less likelihood for admittance to operate in favor of the least favored as a group, e.g., Nina Simone, was denied entrance the famous music conservatory in Philadelphia. Some members of the least favored positions are allowed to cross the barrier erected to deny entrance based on the admission standard of that group, e.g., Collin Powell and Condoleezza Rice.

In other words, those allowed to cross the barrier are declared "qualified" members from the least favored. Stated differently, the possibilities of the removal of barriers that appear before a member of the least favored are nil to minuscule thus allowing only a selected few entrance. Further, entrance may be temporary as many have discovered after they have returned to their old positions e.g., many Rhythm and Blues/Rock and Roll "stars" fell from fame after a brief stay in the music business. A return to the old position is like never entering the new position.

Permanence is only realized when the offspring of the former members of the least favored group are accepted as members by those whose acceptance is considered representing the authority of group entrance. With this in mind, many families of least favored parents devote a life time prep their children to leave their old position, enter a new more advanced position and make allowances so that their offspring will remain there or advance further. These parents are willing to pay the opportunity costs to see their children are invested in as human capital. Epoch discourages or at least minimizes any notions of fairness; access and equality of opportunity that moves those currently in the most favored positions into positions lower than one they currently occupy. Thus relative expansion with proper investments assures the scholar learner invested in will be able to move into a better way of life than that enjoyed by the family at the moment. That idea is only doable in an open society.

What this dialectic or dialogic represents is its contradictions inherent in an open society based on what is required for the most favored to maintain social control. Looking at the current dynamic, the social arrangement of this of the number of members allowed into new more favored positions is one way of keeping its membership current and fluid.

Appendix

A GAME OF CHESS PLAYED OUT IN REAL TIME

IN THE LAW OF POSITION, A POSITION THEORY, The purpose of the Rules of Chess is to explain, i.e., to show, what each character's role on the chess board is in relationship to the two (2) Kings, the black and white positions, i.e., in what manner each character will be allowed to play the game.

Even in game the gender of the second sex is played out as a position. However, one must be careful with that. Queens are the playmakers operating in the background. Clearly, they know what they are doing. Their roles are clearly understood. The Queen occupying the White Position is presented as the most favored of the second sex. She has an advantage over her counterpart the Black Queen representative of the least favored position. Enjoying an advantage over the Black Queen forces the Black Queen to be more creative in her movements, more cautious in her game plan, more cunning in her actions and corresponding activities with the understanding that there appear to be no equals among equals.

According to these rules, the Pawns are the least favored. They represent the peasants, slaves artisans, casual laborers, vagabonds and low life individuals, i.e., the lumpen as members of the under classes of the towns.

Who are the lumpen and what roles do they play? They are the official pawns that are required to suffer the causalities of wars and other organized conflicts conducted by the Kings of the two positions and executed by the Knights. They are the thugs that work with the Rooks with each made to think that members of the least favored least favored family are always expendable. Yet, they operate with power, allied with either of the favored, the Kings.

The players that can go either way, i.e., support or betray the King is the Rook. Played well each Rook serves as the King's handyman. As a group they represent the connivance strata. They watch and tell on anybody for a fee. Their working premise is "everybody can be bought and sold if the price is right."

The Bishops are the representatives of the most favored while always conspiring to take over the monarchy at the proper moment. They get their positions through conquest, slavery, robbery, and sleeping with somebody in the Kings mansions. Thus, they move accordingly, with caution, suspicion, and double speak in maintaining their positions always with eyes focused on the King's position.

Sir Knight is the epitome of the strivers of today. They represent the affluent-poor. They are of the convenience sector, the service strata. They provide whatever is required to carry out the wishes of the King. Their acquired roles are to serve as the buffer between the King, the Barons, and the Peasants. Their motto is "watch your bask, cover your ass, and please watch out for the Rooks."

References

Alinsky, Saul, Twelve (12) rules for Radicals.

Butler, Octavia E. 1979. Kindred. Boston: BeaOcon.

Chase-Riboud, Baraba.1979. Sally Hemings. (A Novel). Chicago: Chicago Review Press 2009.

Cox, Oliver Cromwell, 1970 Caste, Class, and Race: A Study in Social Dynamics. New York: Monthly Review Press.

Craig, William James. (Editor) 1916. The Complete Works of William Shakespeare. (Arranged by Henry M. Pinioned).

Carruthers, Jacob H. 1999. Intellectual Warfare. Chicago: Third World Press.

Cruse, Harold. 1967. The Crisis of the Negro Intellectual: a Historical Analysis of Failure of Black Leadership. New York: Morrow

De Tocqueville, Alexis. (Trans Henry Reeve). Democracy in America.

Du Bois, W.E.B. 1909. The Souls of Black Folk. New York: Dover Publications, Inc,

_____. 1896. The Suppression of the African Slave Trade to the United States 1638-1870. New York Longmans, Greek, and Co.

Dunbar-Ortiz, Roxanne. An Indigenous Peoples History of the United States. ReVisioning America History.

Engels, Fredrich. 1888. The Communist Manifesto [English edition, edited by Fredrich Engels]

Fanon, Franc [trans. Richard Philcox]. 1967. Black Skin White Masks. New York: Grove Press.

_____. 1963. The Wretched of the Earth. New York: Drove Press.

Fazal, Tanisha M. 2007. State Death: The Politics and Geography of Conquest, Occupation, and Annexation. Princeton: Princeton University Press.

Handsberry, Loraine. 1958. A Raison in three Sun. New York: Random House

Henry, Winston, 1973. Strategy for a Black Agenda. New York: International Publishers.

Hunter, Delridge LaVeon. 2019. Death of the Negro: An African American Experience in the Development of Black Popular Culture. NC: Create Space.

James, C.L.R. 1963. The Black Jacobins. Vintage Books.

Kwame, Nkrumah. Neo-Colonialism, the Last Stage of Imperialism. ISBN-13: 978-0717801404. ISBN-10: 0717801403

Lynch, Willie. The Willie Lynch Letter and the Making of a Slave.   [A Fiction]

Marx, Karl. Das Capital.

Machiavelli, Niccolo. 1469-1527. 1982. The Prince. Dover Publications, Inc.

Myrdal Gunnar. 1944. An American Dilemma, Harper Books.

Northup. Solomon. 1854. Twelve Years A Slave. Auburn: Derby and Miller.

Orwell, George. 1945. Animal Farm. New York: Harcourt.

Orwell, George. 1949. 1984. New York: Harcourt.

Rodney, Walter, 1972 (2011. How Europe
Underdeveloped Africa.
Baltimore: Black Classic Press

Silman, I. Jerry. 1998. The Complete Book of Chess
Strategy:
Grandmaster Techniques from A to Z. Los Angeles:
Siles Press.

Smith, Adam. 2015. An Inquiry into the Nature and
Causes of the Wealth of Nations. Irvine, CA: Xist
Publishing.
Sunzi.

Spencer-Brown, G., 1979. Laws of Form.

Stowe, Harriet Beecher. Uncle Tom's Cabin or Life
Among The Lowly. A Public Domain Book.

Wagner, Sally. 2001. Roesch. Sisters in Spirit:
Haudenosaunee (Iroquois) Influence on Early American
Feminists. Summertown, Inn: Native Voices.

Williams, Eric. 1844 (2015). Capitalism and Slavery.
Philadelphia: The Great Library Collection.

Woodson, Carter Godwin. 2010. The Mis-Education of
the Negro. Seven Treasures Publications.